FOREWORD

This is Fr John Murray's third book on the lives of saints. In this volume, his focus is largely on the role the family plays in people's journey towards holiness, as well as on the call to holiness of married couples themselves. The stories told here are remarkable for their variety, and not all of them tell of happy marriages or model families. They all remind us, however, that marriage is a call to personal communion between two people, where in the heart of the family the faith is nurtured and passed on to the next generation.

The lives of the men and women told here have been recognised by many as inspiring manifestations of a living faith in the life, death and resurrection of Christ. Many of the people included have already been officially declared saints by the Church; others, while not officially canonised, have been considered by the faithful to be outstanding in holiness. Thanks to Fr John Murray, these inspiring exemplars of the domestic Church as lived in real time, in concrete circumstances and in a variety of socio-economic situations, will assist many people – couples, grandparents, single uncles and aunts, parish reading groups and countless others – to prepare for the ninth World Meeting of Families which will take place in August 2018 in Dublin.

Long after that event, this little book will stand as a reminder of the call to holiness that Christian marriage entails, and the centrality of the family in passing on the gospel of eternal salvation.

†**Noel Treanor**
Bishop of Down and Connor
Feast of the Holy Family
31 December 2017

D0273473

CONTENTS

ᡧᢀᡧ

—ᡧSS ELIZABETH AND ZECHARIAH ~ 7

—ᡧST JOSEPH ~ 10

—ᡧTHE HOLY INNOCENTS ~ 13

—ᡧST CLARE OF ASSISI (1194–1253) ~ 16

—ᡧBL. MARGARET OF CASTELLO (1287–1320) ~ 20

—ᡧST THOMAS MORE (1478–1535) ~ 24

—ᡧST MARGARET CLITHEROW (1556–86) ~ 28

—ᡧST BENEDICT JOSEPH LABRE (1748–83) ~ 32

—ᡧST LOUIS MARTIN (1823–94) ~ 36
AND ST MARIE-AZÉLIE 'ZÉLIE' GUÉRIN MARTIN (1831–77)

—ᡧVEN. MATT TALBOT (1856–1925) ~ 40

—ᡧST JOSEPHINE BAKHITA (1869–1947) ~ 43

Contents

⁓❦⁓

BL. SOLANUS CASEY (1870–1957) ～ 47

KAROL AND EMILIA WOJTYLA (1879–1941, 1884–1929) ～ 51

JACQUES AND RAÏSSA MARITAIN (1882–1973, 1883–1960) ～ 55

BRIDGET MARY GAVIN (1889–1966) ～ 59

ST MARIA SKOBTSOVA (1891–1945) ～ 62

BL. LAURA VICUÑA (1891–1904) ～ 66

MARY MARTIN (1892–1875) ～ 70

JÓZEF AND WIKTORIA ULMA (1900–44, 1912–44) ～ 74

JÉRÔME LEJEUNE (1926–94) ～ 77

ANTONIA BRENNER (1926–2013) ～ 81

FELIPE AND MARY BARREDA (1931–83, 1933–83) ～ 84

Ss Elizabeth and Zechariah

Elizabeth smiled a little to herself as she clutched her stomach. She could feel life stirring there, feel those kicks that she thought she would never feel. She gently took Zechariah's hand and moved it along her belly until he too could feel the movement. He too broke into a smile.

Zechariah was back home now after having spent several weeks on duty in the Temple in Jerusalem. She had missed him during those weeks away, as she always did. Despite their years of barrenness, he was her rock and she was his. They had each other. This time, however, there was something new happening for them, for she was showing clear signs of her pregnancy. She was wondering how the other women would take the news, since she was 'past the time'. But Zechariah knew that God had blessed them.

Elizabeth was so glad that Mary had come to visit her. Her cousin was almost thirty years younger, and yet she was so wise and caring. Elizabeth did not know what she would have done if the younger woman had not arrived to help her. Indeed, Mary had her own problems. Given her age and situation, tongues had started to wag. After all, she was not yet married to Joseph. Some were disappointed that 'he could not wait', that the carpenter did not respect the 'aw and the customs of their people.

Elizabeth knew from the moment Mary appeared at her door that Joseph was not the father, for her arrival had a strange effect. The baby in her own womb literally leapt within her when Mary appeared at the open door of their house. Elizabeth could scarcely breathe with excitement, for something told her that Mary was carrying someone very special. These thoughts were confirmed when Mary launched into a great prayer of praise. Her words echoed the prayer of Hannah, the mother of Samuel, in the Bible story they all knew well. For those who might have talked, Mary had a message, and that message was to praise God.

Zechariah had so much to say but for some reason he could not speak. Something had happened in the Temple all those weeks ago. He had seen an angel in a vision, who had told him strange things. Zechariah was a believer, of course – after all he had served as a priest in the Temple for many years – but the things the angel told him were simply incredible! He wanted to speak, to tell Elizabeth what he had heard, but he just could not get the words out. He hoped that his silence would come to an end soon. In the meantime, as he watched his wife of many years, he admired the way she was adjusting to her new situation as if this was not her first time. As she set about doing the simple things of the day – washing, cleaning, cooking – he knew that everything was different and that she was different. There was a joy and a peace about her, as if God was totally in charge.

Some people told Zechariah that Elizabeth's age would be against her. They warned that their child might not be as healthy as they would like. He had heard such talk before but knew that God had blessed them with life and God would look after this child's birth.

When the time came for Elizabeth to give birth, all the neighbours gathered around. They were overjoyed that she was able to produce a son. 'He will be just like his father', someone said. 'A new Zechariah', said another. 'He will be able to take his father's place in the Temple', another suggested. 'God is gracious,' a loud voice said suddenly, 'and that will be his name. His name will be John.' Everyone looked at the speaker in amazement, for they had not heard Zechariah speak for months. A great hush came over them, and some began to wonder at what was happening. 'Who will this child turn out to be?' they asked.

And now Zechariah, the old priest who had not spoken for so long, launched into his own great hymn of praise, giving vent to all the energy and frustration he had felt during his months of silence. 'And you, my child, shall be called a prophet of the Most High, for you shall go before the Lord to prepare the way for him' (*Lk. 1:76*).

At that moment, the two proud parents could never have imagined just how John would turn out!

St Joseph

Joseph is the silent one in the gospel but he is not the only one who remained silent! For centuries, the Church paid Joseph scant attention out of concern to affirm the divine fatherhood of Jesus and the role of Mary in the history of salvation. So, the one who was without a word in the gospels remained without a word in the Church for many centuries. It wasn't until the sixteenth century that a cult began to appear, and it wasn't until 1870 that Pope Pius IX (1792–1878) declared him Patron of the Universal Church.

Joseph appears in the Gospels of Luke and Matthew but differently in each. These differences can be explained by the contrasting theological interests of the two evangelists. Both tell us that Joseph was betrothed in marriage to Mary, and was found to be pregnant before they came together. After that, Luke's version emphasises Mary's perspective, showing how Mary's 'yes' enabled God's plan to unfold and for Jesus to be born. Many centuries later, St Bernard of Clairvaux would write beautifully that 'the whole of creation held its breath waiting for Mary's response'.

In Matthew's Gospel the story is told from Joseph's point of view. At a distance of two millennia, and in today's very different moral environment, it is hard for us to appreciate the quandary in which Joseph found himself. Mary's pregnancy preceded any divine reassurance. The text delicately avoids the option Joseph could have taken – stoning to death – as suggested so graphically in the Old Testament (*Deut.22:21*). Instead, we read that Joseph 'being an upright man and wanting to spare her disgrace, decided to divorce her informally' (*Mt.1:19*). In speaking of Joseph here, Matthew uses a special Greek work *dikaios*, which can best be translated as 'a man of honour' or 'a righteous man'. We will soon see how appropriate that word is.

Matthew also emphasises the Jewish perspective in his Gospel, which is typical of his concerns. His Gospel quotes the Old Testament more frequently than the others – twenty-eight times in all – because he wants to show that Jesus is the fulfilment of the prophecies, the long-awaited Messiah of Israel. Like the other Joseph in the Old Testament – the son of Jacob, the 'dreamer' sold by his brothers into slavery – Matthew shows Joseph receiving God's plan for the salvation of Israel and the whole world in a dream.

That dream changed Joseph's plan completely. In it he saw an angel, telling him not to be afraid but to take Mary home as his wife, because it was through the Holy Spirit that she had conceived. Joseph heard and he obeyed, taking Mary to his home as his wife, even though he knew that tongues would wag and his own virtue would be questioned. Joseph is indeed a man of honour; he is also a man of faith and a man of courage.

Readers will know that Joseph has two feasts in the Church calendar, on 19 March and 1 May. The second of these celebrates the fact that Joseph was a worker: a carpenter. It is a celebration of the 'hidden gospel', those years in which the creator of the universe – the *Pantokrator* of the icons – passed his time quietly mending tables and fixing chairs under the guidance of Joseph. Through those years,

Joseph reminds us that we are saved more often through our fidelity to the simple, humdrum things of life, than through the dramatic, exciting events we – and history – like to remember.

Joseph was a simple man of Nazareth, too poor to afford more than the cheapest offering when he brought his son to the Temple for circumcision. His lowly background sometimes made him the butt of other people's jokes. The more sophisticated people dismissed Jesus at one stage as 'the carpenter's son', and Nathanael wondered at his first encounter with Jesus, 'Can anything good come out of Nazareth?'

Pope St John Paul II (1920–2005) honoured Joseph in a beautiful apostolic exhortation in 1989, *Redemptoris custos* ('guardian of the Redeemer'). Joseph is the one who sought shelter for Mary when she was about to give birth. He is the one who, with divine guidance, sought to bring his two beloved charges far away from the menaces of Herod. He is the one who joined Mary in their desperate search for Jesus when the pilgrimage to Jerusalem didn't work out as planned. The words of Mary after they found Jesus in the Temple 'your father and I have been worried' scarcely convey the emotions they must have felt on that occasion. Jesus' reply, 'I must be about my Father's business' suggested perfectly Joseph's role in the divine plan. He was to be the steward, the guardian, looking after Jesus until he began to exercise his own ministry as saviour and teacher.

Joseph, righteous man, holder of dreams, spouse of Mary, guardian of the Redeemer, pray for us.

THE HOLY INNOCENTS

'See that you do not despise any of these little ones; for I tell you their angels in heaven continually see the face of my heavenly father' (*Mt.18:10*).

The timing of the Feast of the Holy Innocents, a few days after Christmas, can often seem strange to us: as if breaking into the peace and goodwill of the festive season, and even invading the somewhat selfish contentment of our secular celebrations. Indeed, even before that, on the day after Christmas, we are asked to call to mind another tragic event, the killing of Stephen, the first martyr. It is as if the Lord is saying to us, 'Do you want to follow me? Then be prepared for trials'.

We know the story, of course. To ensure that he would eliminate the new-born king, whom he saw as a threat, Herod killed all the boys in the area who were two years old and under. We don't know how many were killed; estimates vary from a few score to fourteen thousand. The latter figure appeared in the Byzantine liturgy, while the Copts put the number even higher at 144,000. These numbers were probably intended to be more symbolic than actual. More sober assessments suggest that around twenty-six children were killed in the town itself, with another twelve or so in the outlying areas.

Such atrocities were not unthinkable, given Herod's character. He drowned his sixteen-year-old brother-in-law, killed his uncle, aunt and mother-in-law, and murdered his own two sons and some three hundred officials whom he accused of siding with his sons. To suggest he was paranoid is an understatement. He simply did not brook opposition.

The innocent children who were killed were not believers in the strict sense, of course, but nonetheless they were killed for the sake of Christ, and from the third century the Church has seen them as martyrs. By the fourth century the feast was celebrated in North Africa and it had spread to the universal church by the sixth century. In early times the festival commemorated all newly baptised infants who had died prematurely, thus linking the sacrament not just to Easter but also to Christmas. That particular understanding of the feast is returning again in some areas, as parents call to mind their stillborn children, and those who had not reached the age of maturity.

The event as described in Scripture has given rise to many different representations. Medieval dramas included this story among the events portrayed. One such was *The Pageant of the Shearmen and the Tailors*, which was performed in England and included a haunting song which in time became known as the 'Coventry Carol'. Matthew in his Gospel account had already anticipated this kind of lamentation by his plaintive quotation from the prophet Jeremiah, 'a voice is heard in Ramah, weeping and great mourning, Rachel weeping for her children and refusing to be consoled, because they are no more' (*Mt.2:17*).

Artists and painters too have captured the scene, sometimes interpreting it in the light of contemporary events. Painting in the period of the religious wars following the Reformation, Bruegel's versions show the soldiers who killed the children carrying banners of the time. Nicolas Poussin painted the scene in 1634 at the height of the Thirty Years War. Peter Paul Rubens and Guido Reni also painted the scene in dramatic detail.

Liturgically, the Anglican and Lutheran communions remember not just children on this day but indeed all victims of injustice who have paid the ultimate price for their innocence. The list could be endless and the numbers are beyond imagining but the following can readily be called to mind: the six million Jewish people massacred in the Holocaust; the hundreds of thousands of people fire-bombed in the carpet bombing of Dresden and other German cities at the end of the war; the countless numbers of African slaves transported to America and the Indies; the victims of Pol Pot in the Killing Fields of Cambodia; the millions sacrificed on the altar of Communism in Russia and China and beyond; the victims of the atom bombs of Hiroshima and Nagasaki in 1945. There have been millions and millions of innocents, mostly unknown to history except as cold statistics. We can be grateful that they are all known to God.

In recent decades, we have added another category to the Holy Innocents: the millions of unborn children who are sadly killed through abortion before they see the light of day. Let's pray that, whatever public opinion may hold and whatever laws are passed, we as Christians can remain firmly on the side of life, at every stage of its existence.

The feast of the Holy Innocents is not simply a memorial to those who died before their time. While the little children of Bethlehem were unconscious victims of forces beyond their control, they also serve to remind us of the many who dream of a different future. In remembering the Holy Innocents, we commemorate the victims of Herod's rage. But we also celebrate Herod's failure, for the child of hope lives on in every generation.

St Clare of Assisi
(1194–1253)

St Clare of Assisi is the patron saint of television and eye disease, good weather and needle workers. A surprising mix of patronages for someone who remained in her convent for over fifty years! Everyone knows about St Francis of Assisi, a saint loved by all denominations and generations, but less well known is Chiara Offreduccio, who became Francis's first female disciple and bequeathed to the Church an order of sisters which survives to this day. In English, we know her as St Clare, and the order she founded are called the 'Poor Clares'.

Before she entered religious life, Clare was something of a celebrity. If she were alive today, she would probably be seen in the pages of *Hello* magazine, or its Italian equivalent, *Oggi*. She was rich and beautiful, and had many suitors. She came from noble stock, and her relatives, particularly her father, had high hopes for her future. An arranged marriage with some nobleman's son would do wonders for his own prestige and position in the world. Already in her teens, she had refused two proposals of marriage; girls were married very young in those days.

In her teenage years, Clare already had a strong faith but she had not yet found her vocation. In 1212, at the age of eighteen, she heard St Francis preach a Lenten sermon in her parish church, and she was riveted. She had never heard anything like it. Still, she was wise enough to realise that her goal in life was not to be a reflection of Francis but to be a reflection of Christ. 'Christ is the way,' she said, 'and Francis showed it to me.'

She left home secretly on the evening of Palm Sunday, making her way through the olive groves and dark fields to the Church of St Mary of the Angels, where she met St Francis and his brothers. Before the altar she laid aside her fine clothes and put on a penitential habit, while St Francis cut her beautiful long hair as a sign of her espousal to Christ. It was a radical step.

Initially Clare's family tried to convince her of the folly of her actions. The story of St Francis, himself the son of a rich merchant, had spread far and wide, and while many respected him for his radical commitment to the gospel there were others who saw him as a misguided fool who had deeply embarrassed his father. Now, Clare's family feared that they might suffer that embarrassment.

St Francis arranged for Clare to stay in a nearby Benedictine convent but within a few days her family had tracked her down. They pleaded with her to return to the family home, and when this proved fruitless they tried to drag her there by force. Clare finally stopped them by tearing off her veil to reveal her shorn head. They stepped back in shock. She was already 'one of them'.

Soon afterwards, Clare's sister joined her, and so began the order that was to become a contemplative sisterhood within the Church. Later, and after the death of her husband, Clare's mother joined her daughters in the convent. The Church of San Damiano became the focal point for Clare's new order. Unlike the Franciscan friars who moved around the countryside to preach, Clare's sisters lived in enclosure, since an itinerant life was not conceivable for women at that time. Their life consisted of prayer and manual work, as indeed it does to this day.

Initially, the order was directed by St Francis himself but in 1216 Clare accepted the role of abbess of San Damiano. She was a gentle but strong leader, defending her order from the interference of bishops who wanted to impose a rule resembling that of St Benedict rather than St Francis's more rigorous approach. Indeed, Clare sought to imitate St Francis's way of life so closely that she was sometimes called *alter Franciscus*, 'another Francis'. In his latter days she nursed him during his illnesses, until his death in 1226.

Clare is frequently depicted carrying a monstrance. The origin of that image goes back to an incident that happened in her life in 1234. The army of Frederick the Second, Holy Roman Emperor (1194–1250) was devastating the valley of Spoleto not far from Assisi. One night, his soldiers scaled the walls of San Damiano. Hearing the noise, Clare calmly rose from her bed and, taking the monstrance with the sacred host, proceeded to face the window where the soldiers were entering. As she raised the Blessed Sacrament, the soldiers fell back as if dazzled, and those behind them took to flight.

It was Pope Pius XII (1876–1958) who nominated Clare as the patron saint of television, and it too goes back to a story told about the saint. It is said that one time, when she was sick in bed and could not attend Mass in the convent chapel, she prayed to be able to participate as fully as possible in the celebration. In response to her prayer the Lord allowed her to see the entire Mass on the wall of her cell. Just like a plasma screen!

After St Francis's death, Clare continued to promote the growth of the order, thwarting every attempt to dilute their commitment to radical poverty. She persisted with these efforts, despite periods of ill health, until finally she had the satisfaction of Pope Innocent IV's

(1195–1254) decision that her rule would serve as the governing rule for the order. Two days later, on 11 August, Clare died at the age of fifty-nine. Within two years she was canonised. A new basilica was completed in 1260, and her remains were transferred to it and interred underneath the high altar.

A few years ago, I found myself in the company of a good priest friend. We were in Assisi and he wanted to visit the Poor Clare convent. He remembered visiting there some thirty years before in the company of his mother, shortly after his ordination. We rang the bell and asked for the sister he remembered from that time. She arrived, in her late sixties now, but still alive and full of zeal. 'I am as happy now as the day I entered,' she told us. I was struck by those words. What a wonderful testimony to the religious life and to the great witness of St Clare over eight centuries earlier!

BL. MARGARET OF CASTELLO
(1287–1320)

Heroes! We all have heroes. We need them to challenge us and give us purpose. For many people today, their heroes are the gladiators who bestride the stadiums of the world's great football teams: Ronaldo, Messi, Pogba, Kane. Others might look nearer to home for their heroes, whether in Gaelic football or rugby or some other sport.

I admire all of the above but as a priest who visits the sick and the housebound at least once a month, many of my heroes are much nearer to hand. I am constantly amazed at the love and devotion I find as I do my rounds. As I spend a few minutes with Cormac bringing him Communion, I marvel at the devotion of his mother; because of his paralysed state, she has to nurse him, lift him and cater for his every need all the time.

I want to write here about another hero of mine, a saint about whom little is known and whose name few will recognise. Margaret of Castello lived from 1287 to 1320, and she is the patron saint of the disabled.

Parisio and Emilia were well-to-do gentry in the region of Florence, in the Tuscan part of Italy. They had planned a great celebration for the birth of their child, their first. When the event happened, however, there were no celebrations and there was no great feast. Their child was born blind and deformed, with one leg considerably shorter than the other. Her parents were totally shocked, and could find no room in their hearts for their little daughter. 'How could this be?' they wondered. 'Why did God allow this to happen?' Deciding to hide the child and tell no one about her, they gave her to a servant girl to care for secretly. 'What is her name?' the servant asked. 'She has no name' was the reply, and so the servant baptised the child Margaret, a name derived from the word for 'pearl'.

It is perhaps easy today for us to be critical of Parisio and Emilia and their attitude to their daughter. In those times there was no real understanding of the place of disabled people in the lives of others. They put them out of sight. Yet, eight centuries after Margaret's birth, many people still have no room in the inn for those who are disabled.

Margaret remained shut away from the world, living as she did in a small cell adjacent to the family chapel. Here she received the sacraments and it was from the family chaplain that she came to know about God. She remained in this tiny enclosure until she was sixteen years of age, when her parents took her to a Franciscan shrine in the town of Castello, hoping for a miracle. When none came – at least none that they could see – they abandoned her in the streets of the town and left for home, never to see her again.

Margaret was now at the mercy of passers-by as she begged for food and shelter. Eventually some Dominican nuns took her in and helped her to survive. In time, she became a member of the Dominican Third Order as a *mantellata*, meaning that she wore the religious habit and veil, and she spent the rest of her short life in prayer and works of charity. Despite her difficulties, Margaret remained serene, cheerful and courageous, never becoming bitter, although she had every reason to be. She never complained and never reproached others. Discouragement was simply a word she did not know. Each day she found her strength in Holy Communion and in her prayer.

Above all, Margaret looked at her suffering through the eyes of faith. She did not know why God had allowed her to have so many afflictions but she knew in her heart that God was a loving Father who never permits misfortune without some good reason and who always turns evil to good for his children. She even wondered why people pitied her; was it not a privilege to suffer for Christ?

Indeed, her very suffering made her more open to the needs of others. Often Margaret would visit prisoners and the sick, and she would be present especially when people were near to death. As with many of the saints, her practical care and attention often manifested itself in miraculous cures and healings. Once, when visiting a man in prison whose heart was full of hatred, her body was lifted up in his presence and remained suspended above the ground for several minutes. Needless to say, the man was moved, expressed contrition and made his peace with God.

Bl. Margaret died on 13 April 1320 at the age of thirty-three. Sadly, even in death she was treated as an outcast. The people cried out for her to be buried in a tomb inside the church but the priest protested. When a little girl who was crippled was healed through her intercession, however, the people had their way. Indeed, since her death over 200 miracles have been attributed to her intercession. In 1558 her remains were transferred because her coffin was rotten. Inside the coffin her clothes had similarly rotted but her body was preserved, and remains incorrupt to this day.

In 1609 Pope Paul V (1550–1621) beatified her but the final stage of the process of canonisation remains to be complete. And so, today, an unwanted daughter is one of the glories of the Church and a figure of inspiration for those who carry blemishes or imperfections in their bodies. Her incorrupt body can be seen in the chapel of the School for the Blind in Castello, Italy. Her feast day is 13 April.

ST THOMAS MORE
(1478–1535)

'Become a teacher, Richard; become a good teacher!' That was the advice St Thomas More gave to a wayward young man, Richard Rich, in the film *A Man for All Seasons*, written by Robert Bolt more than forty years ago. 'But who would know?' Richard wondered. 'Well, first of all,' More replied, 'your pupils would know; and you would know; and then God would know – and that is not a bad audience.' Sadly, Richard did not listen to his mentor's wisdom, and in the end he was instrumental in his betrayal, as we will see.

Thomas More was one of the most eminent men of his age. Trained in law, he quickly made his way up the ladder of success to become Lord Chancellor of England in 1529. It was the highest position a layman could attain in the land. Erasmus of Rotterdam, like More a remarkable scholar and humanist, remarked about More's appointment, 'Happy the commonwealth where kings appoint such officials'.

The trappings of his position mattered little to More. Often bribes would come his way, with the intention of influencing his judgement but he treated these with contempt. In his youth, he had considered a vocation to the monastic life, but he decided to study and practice law instead. He lived his Christian faith as a layman to the fullest possible extent, attending Mass daily, praying frequently and even wearing a hair shirt as penance beneath his fine robes.

In his family life, Thomas was blessed with children, and when his first wife, Jane, died at a young age, he quickly remarried. He found in Alice, who was four years his senior, a loyal wife and an excellent stepmother to his children. As time went on, she began to find herself frustrated by his anxious questioning but no one loved him more.

King Henry VIII found More to be a wise choice for the responsible role he had given him. He often sought his counsel, and Thomas served the King with complete devotion and absolute loyalty. But, despite appearances, all was not well. Storm clouds were gathering on the horizon as the winds of the Reformation began to sweep across the channel to England.

In his early years as king, Henry emphatically proclaimed his loyalty to the Church's teaching. In 1521, he published an answer to Luther's criticisms and had, in consequence, been honoured by the Pope with the title 'Defender of the Faith'. Personal issues, however, were about to surface in Henry's life, giving rise to serious theological disputes. Henry had become unfaithful to his wife, Catherine of Aragon, and he wanted to marry his young mistress, Anne Boleyn. For this, he wanted the Pope to declare his marriage to Catherine null and void. The Pope refused, upholding the sanctity of the original marriage, a decision Henry rejected. Caught between the two authorities, Thomas found himself in an impossible position and felt he had to resign as Chancellor.

He retired to his home and declined to attend the coronation of the new queen. He was hoping all the time to sit out the storm until the ship of government settled into calmer waters. In 1534, two years after his resignation, a new Act of Succession was introduced. Thomas was willing to accept the substance of the act, which required Henry's loyal subjects to accept the offspring of the new queen as true successors to the throne, but there was a coda to the act which proved to be a stumbling block. This coda declared Henry's original marriage to be null and void; this was a step too far for More.

He soon found himself in the tower of London, which for fifteen months was to be his final home. Pressure mounted on him from all sides. The court tried to convince him to take the oath of allegiance as required. His family tried to persuade him to 'say the words' which would free him to return to them. In reply to Alice's attempts to coax him to change course, he replied with typical wit, 'My good woman, you are no good at business. Do you really want me to exchange eternity for twenty years?'

Prison life, with its cold, hunger and vermin, took its toll on Thomas, but he retained his dignity throughout his ordeal. One lovely story is told of his time in prison. Thomas got quite close to one of his jailers, and one day he asked the jailer, 'Do you want to know a secret?' The poor man was excited, thinking that he was going to be given access to the famous man's supposed wealth. Instead, Thomas quoted a piece from St John's Gospel: 'Eternal life is this, to know you the only true God, and Jesus Christ whom you have sent' (Jn. 17:3). As far as Thomas was concerned this was the only treasure that he needed.

On 1 February 1535, a further act was passed by parliament proclaiming the king as the head of the Church in England. Thomas maintained his silence about this act but nevertheless he was brought to trial and accused of treason. Sadly, it was Richard Rich, the young man whom Thomas had advised to be a teacher, who denounced Thomas by perjuring himself. Thomas was convicted and sentenced to death.

On 6 May, he was taken to the place of execution and, though the months of prison had worn him down, he still maintained his famous wit and composure. To the guard accompanying him he said, 'I pray you, see me safe up, and as for my coming down let me shift for myself!' His final words were to the bystanders of whom there were many that day. 'I die in and for the faith of the holy Catholic Church. Pray for me in this world and I shall pray for you in that world. Pray for the King that it please God to send him good counsellors. I die as the King's true servant but God's first.'

St Thomas More was canonised in 1935, and his feast is celebrated, together with that of another martyr of those troubled times, Archbishop John Fisher, on 22 June.

St Margaret Clitherow
(1556–86)

'The blood of the martyrs is the seed of the Church.' These words were written a long time ago, in the second century of the Christian era, by a great and influential author, Tertullian (155–240). He spoke from the experience of his own time, which witnessed the periodically severe persecution of Christians. Every century since has come to verify the truth of his statement. In our own time, we can think of the fifty-seven Iraqi Christians who were killed a few years ago as they gathered to celebrate the Eucharist or the twenty-two Coptic Christians who were beheaded on a beach in Libya in 2015. Some commentators suggest that more Christians may have been killed in the last hundred years than in all the previous nineteen centuries.

St Margaret Clitherow was the first woman to be martyred for the Catholic faith during the reign of Queen Elizabeth I (1533–1603). She was the daughter of a wealthy merchant in the city of York, and she married John Clitherow, a prosperous butcher and widower, when she was just sixteen. Though raised in the recently established Church of England, Margaret soon converted to

Catholicism, apparently inspired by the courage and sufferings of so many Catholics during those repressive times. Tertullian would have understood.

Although Margaret's husband remained in the Church of England, he continued to love and cherish his wife, even when the choice she had made in those difficult days brought danger to his house. The couple had two children of their own, and Margaret also helped to raise her husband's children from his previous marriage, seeing to it that they were all raised in the Catholic faith. Later, two of the sons would become priests and one daughter a nun. Her husband once said of her, 'Let them take all I have and save her, for she is the best wife in all England, and the best Catholic'.

Margaret helped John with his business, and was popular among his customers, including those who did not share her faith. She was an exemplary witness to this faith, praying each day for an hour and a half, attending Mass whenever the opportunity arose and fasting four times a week. As the persecution of Catholics intensified, however, it became more difficult for Margaret and others like her to practise their faith.

On several occasions, Margaret was imprisoned for not attending the local service of the Church of England, once for a period of two years. She used those times to become better acquainted with the gospels and to read *The Imitation of Christ* by Thomas à Kempis. She claimed that, were it not for the love of her family, she would gladly have stayed in prison, where she enjoyed the company of other Catholics and where she also learned to read and write.

In 1585, an additional law was passed which made it high treason for a Catholic priest to live in England, and a crime for anyone to harbour or aid a Catholic priest. The penalty for breaking this law was death. Despite the risk involved, Margaret welcomed priests into her home, sheltering them when in danger in a disguised 'priest's hole'. These hiding places were a common feature of Catholic homes in Elizabethan England, many of them the creation of a Jesuit brother, Nicholas Owen, now himself a saint. 'By God's grace,' Margaret wrote, 'all priests shall be more welcome to me than ever they were, and I will do what I can to set forward God's Catholic service.'

Margaret's home became one of the most important hiding places for fugitive priests in the north of England. When the authorities discovered that Margaret intended to send her son, Henry, to a Catholic school in France, her house was searched and various Catholic objects were found, including books and vestments for Mass. They also discovered the 'priest's hole' but no priest was found there. Margaret was arrested, but she refused to plead guilty or agree to trial by jury. 'Having made no offence, I need no trial,' she argued. English law decreed that anyone who refused such a trial should be 'pressed to death', and that was the terrible punishment meted out to Margaret.

On the morning of 25 March 1586, having sewn her own shroud during the night and having prayed for the pope, the clergy and the queen, Margaret was taken to the place of execution. It was a cruel death. She was made to lie sandwiched between a rock and a large wooden slab. Then weights were placed upon the slab one by one, until such time as she could no longer breathe. She was crushed to death. She did not cry out during the ordeal but quietly prayed 'Jesu, Jesu, have mercy upon me'. She was only thirty years of age, and it was Good Friday.

After her death, her remains were left for six hours before the weights were removed. A bystander severed her hand at this time, and this relic is now housed in the chapel of the Bar Convent in the city of York. People were in shock at the brutal killing of this good woman. Queen Elizabeth herself wrote to the citizens of the city expressing her horror at the death of a fellow woman. We can only marvel at the faith and courage of 'the pearl of York', as she is known.

Pope Paul VI (1897–1978) canonised her in 1970, along with a group of other martyrs of the period.

ST BENEDICT JOSEPH LABRE
(1748–83)

I was late for evening prayer, and so as I entered the chapel I tried to slip in without making too much noise. My brother priests, who like me were on retreat, had already begun to recite the psalms. I was happy to see that there was an empty seat at the end of a row. I sat down and began to join in the chant. Then I became aware of the man beside me, not because of anything he did but because of the overpowering smell which came from him. It was so strong I could scarcely breathe. As I found out later, he was a 'gentleman of the road' who had wandered in and had sat down to join in the prayers. I would like to tell you that, like Martin of Tours, I divided my coat in two and gave him half or, like Francis of Assisi, I embraced him at the end but I did neither. When the prayers were over I moved quickly away, although I think I said a few words of greeting to him before I did so.

I tell this story against myself. It happened some years ago, and I hope that God has changed me for the better in the meantime. When I think of it now, however, I realise that my reaction to that man might well have been the same as the reaction of many when they met the saint known as Benedict Joseph Labre. He probably evoked similar feelings of disgust in people who encountered him.

St Benedict was born in 1748 near Boulogne in France, the eldest of fifteen children. His parents were respectable people, held in high regard by all who knew them. There were some priests on both sides of the family. From an early age, Benedict was attracted to the monastic life, and he told his parents that he wished to join the austere branch of the Cistercians at La Trappe. Because of the severity of their rule, his parents were against this step, and Benedict acceded to their wishes. He felt they would come around to his way of thinking in time.

At this time Benedict was particularly close to one of his uncles, Fr Francis, who was his guide and confidant. When a severe epidemic broke out in the area in the summer of 1766, both nephew and uncle were fully occupied bringing practical help and spiritual succour to those afflicted by the disease. Sadly, Francis died as a result of his exertions, and Benedict lost a friend and advisor.

Benedict returned to his earlier idea of entering the Trappist community but was refused. He was likewise turned away by a number of other religious communities. Discouraged by these failures, he concluded that his true vocation was to seek a cloister within the world. Accordingly, he set off by foot on a pilgrimage that lasted several years, wandering thousands of miles across Europe and taking in many of the principal shrines and churches on the way. He dressed in rags and never bathed. This certainly discouraged human contact and contributed to the prayerful isolation which he relished. At the same time, he declined to beg, though passers-by often were moved to give him alms. When he ran out of food, he simply lived off what he might find at the side of the road.

His appearance was as likely to evoke contempt as pity, and he was indeed frequently harassed. Nevertheless, Benedict accepted all this in a spirit of humility. When a priest in confession once asked him if he had ever studied theology Benedict replied, 'Father, I am only a poor beggar'. Those who were able to see beneath his dishevelled appearance, including eventually his confessor, recognised the saint in their midst.

Eventually Benedict settled in Rome where he spent his nights sleeping in the ruins of the Colosseum, where many of the early Christians had been martyred. He spent his days praying in many of the beautiful churches of the city. When his health began to fail, he consented to sleep in a hospice for the destitute. This belated concession to human frailty could not reverse the damage done to his health, however, and at the age of thirty-five he collapsed on the steps of a church and was carried to a nearby house. There he died on 16 April 1783. Almost immediately the local children took up the cry, 'The saint is dead! The saint is dead!' His reputation spread rapidly throughout the city and then to the rest of Europe. It was through one of the accounts of his life that his parents – still alive at this time – heard of the whereabouts of their lost son. He was canonised in 1883.

What lessons can we, who live in a world of designer labels and fast food, draw from such a life? What can he teach us in our world, where appearances and soundbites mean so much to so many people? Maybe he can remind us to *see* that man or woman whom we pass on the street down town, to spare ten seconds to look into those eyes the next time we drop a few coins into the plastic cup. Maybe he can remind us to take a few minutes to share a few words, to ask for a name, to talk about the situation they find themselves in. Who knows, we might even be meeting another Benedict Joseph.

Many years ago, I had the privilege of hearing Mother Teresa at a gathering of priests which I attended. She shared many stories of the suffering she encountered in the streets and the compassionate care of her sisters. She surprised us when she said at one stage that often there was more poverty in the streets of London or New York than in Calcutta. Then she gave an example. Once, while walking through the streets of London, a hand shot out from a doorway, looking for money. She carried none, but instead took the hand in hers and held it for a while. Then the voice from the doorway said, 'It's been such a long time since I felt the warmth of a human hand, such a long time'. May we be privileged to meet St Benedict somewhere today.

St Louis Martin
(1823–94)

and St Marie-Azélie 'Zélie' Guérin Martin
(1831–77)

On 18 October 2015, a married couple were canonised together for the first time in the history of the Church. Appropriately, the ceremony took place at the end of the second session of the Synod of Bishops on the Family, which subsequently prompted Pope Francis to write his Apostolic Exhortation on marriage and the family, *Amoris Laetitia* ('The Joy of Love'). It was a fitting culmination to a synod which had been looking at the whole area of love and relationships in the Christian family.

Readers will be familiar with the story of St Thérèse of Lisieux (1873–1897). Her feast is celebrated on 1 October each year. Most Catholic churches have a statue or a picture of the young Carmelite nun who entered the convent at the age of sixteen and died just eight years later. Like many others who pursued similar vocations, her story might have gone unnoticed but for the notes that her superior had asked her to make and which in time became the best-selling book, *The Story of a Soul*. Upon the publication of this book, there was a universal call from the Catholic world for her canonisation, and this was duly answered within a quarter century of her death.

St Thérèse's parents, Ss Louis Martin and Zélie Guérin Martin, were born in France in the early part of the nineteenth century. Both had desires to enter religious life but they were refused: Louis because of his failure to master Latin and Zélie because of ill health. Louis settled down to become a watchmaker and Zélie became a successful lace maker. The couple met in 1858, and fell in love immediately. Within three months they were married.

We know from their letters that the couple were deeply in love. When he was away, Louis wrote messages to Zélie, signing them, 'Your husband and true friend who loves you for life'. In reply, Zélie once wrote, 'I follow you in spirit all day long; I long to be close to you, my dear Louis; I love you with all my heart, and I feel my affection doubled by being in your presence. I could not live apart from you.'

It might come as a surprise to us to learn that Louis and Zélie chose to live a life of continence for the first year of their marriage. Though not altogether unusual at that time, the sacrifice involved, when made as a mutual decision, was never meant to weaken the marital bond, nor did it for Louis and Zélie. On the advice of their confessor, they went on to begin a family and to have nine children. 'I love children like crazy,' Zélie would say 'I was born to be a mother.' Louis too delighted in his children, giving each one a special name.

Sadly, four of their children died in infancy. The loss was acutely felt by both parents. 'When I closed the eyes of my dear little children,' said Louis, 'and buried them, I felt sorrow through and through. People said to me, "It would have been better never to have had them". I could not stand such language. My children were not lost forever. Life is short and full of miseries, and we shall see our little ones again.' The remaining five children – all girls – one by one entered religious life.

From the outside, there was nothing remarkable about the Martin household. For nineteen years, they lived modestly but comfortably, reaching out to the poor and the needy of their town. Each day, Louis led the family in prayer, of which the rosary was a stable part. And, of course, they also had their times of fun and games.

Then, tragedy struck. In 1877, Zélie was diagnosed with breast cancer and passed away at the young age of forty-five. Following his great loss, Louis decided to make a break with the family home in Alençon, and he and the girls moved to the little town of Lisieux, which was not far away. Then, one by one, the sisters left home, each one seeking her vocation in the seclusion of Carmel. Louis said to a friend, 'it is a great honour for me that the good Lord desires to take all of my children. If I had anything better, I would not hesitate to offer it to him.'

Though lonely, and occasionally suffering from depression, Louis was contented at heart. On one occasion, he confided in his daughters that he was reconsidering his life. Sitting in church one day, he said this prayer, 'My God, I am too happy. It's not possible to go to heaven like that. I want to suffer something for you.' The desire to share in the sufferings of Christ was typical of the spirituality of those days, and his daughters understood that their father was offering himself to the Lord as a 'victim soul'. Indeed, some years later, St Thérèse too would offer herself as a victim to the merciful love of God, as she tells in the entry in her notes for 9 June 1895.

Louis's final years were marked by many health problems. His suffering included a period of three years in the Bon Sauveur psychiatric hospital in Caen. He was diagnosed as having cerebral arteriosclerosis (a hardening of the walls of the arteries) and it was having a deteriorating effect on him. Yet, somehow, he maintained a serene and peaceful outlook. No one who visited him came away sad but rather was edified by his resignation and the way he accepted God's will in his life. He passed away peacefully on 29 July 1894.

St Thérèse herself beautifully testified to the impact of Ss Louis and Zélie's faith on their children shortly before her own death, when she wrote, 'God gave me a father and a mother more worthy of heaven than of earth'.

VEN. MATT TALBOT
(1856–1925)

'I'm going to take the pledge,' Matt suddenly said to his mother. She was beginning to wonder what was the matter with her son for, unusually, he had remained in the house after they had eaten their simple meal. Normally, he couldn't wait for the plates to be cleared so that he could make his way to the pub. 'Go in God's name,' she said, 'but don't take it unless you are going to keep it.' 'I'll go – in God's name,' Matt replied. Then, as he closed the door, his mother added quietly under her breath, 'God give you strength to keep it'.

Matt left the house and walked to Clonliffe, an area of Dublin city close to where he lived. He made his confession and took the pledge for three months. It lasted forty-one years, and he never broke it.

Ven. Matt Talbot was born in 1856. As the child of a poor family, he had to forego any hope of education, and after a year of somewhat basic schooling he started work for a wine merchant at the age of twelve. His father was already an alcoholic, and this family weakness, together with his work environment, did not augur well for Matt. He was already drinking heavily by the time he reached his thirteenth birthday.

Each day, as soon as work was over, Matt and his friends dashed as quickly as they could to the pub, where they would spend most of the rest of the day until closing time. Matt spent every penny he had on drink, and even once pawned his boots for a drink. Once, too, he stole a fiddle from a street musician for the same purpose. Strangely enough, his habit did not prevent him putting in a good day's work during all the years of heavy drinking. In the midst of all this, he even managed an occasional Hail Mary. Indeed, later he would say that he thought Our Lady had something to do with his conversion.

One day in 1884, by which time Matt was twenty-eight years old, something changed. He had been out of work for several days, and he expected his mates would call and take him down to the pub, as usual. When they failed to turn up, he made the decision that would change his life. That decision, originally made for three months, would last for forty-one years, as we have seen. Facing such a radical change in his life, Matt knew that he had to fill the vacuum with something else. And so began a life of prayer and penance that would continue until the day he died.

Having made his confession, and after an absence from the sacraments of several of years, he began to attend an early morning Mass at five o'clock, before proceeding to begin work an hour later. It was a practice he was to continue for the rest of his life. Also, at the end of the working day, he would regularly walk to a church some distance away from his former drinking friends – St Joseph's in Berkeley Road or St Peter's in Phibsboro – and remain there until bedtime.

The early days were tough. During the first three months he once told his mother that he would probably go back to the drink, such was the strength of the 'inner demon'. But he didn't. Indeed, when Fr Paul Cullen, a Jesuit priest who worked in the centre of the city, began the Pioneer Total Abstinence Association in 1898 Matt was one of its first members.

In addition to the daily Masses which Matt attended, there was also another side to his spiritual life: the practice of great mortification. Matt slept on a plank bed with a piece of timber for his pillow. He also slept in chains, which he wore around his leg and on his body for fourteen years before his death. His meals too were frugal, and any surplus money he had he gave to the poor or to the missions. Often he prayed at night from two to four o'clock in the morning, after which he dressed and prepared to make his way for early morning Mass in St Francis Xavier's Church in Gardiner Street.

On 8 June 1925, the *Irish Independent* noted that 'an elderly man collapsed in Granby Lane yesterday. He died later in Jervis Street hospital. There was nothing to indicate his identity'. Matt died as he had lived, anonymously. Burial followed a few days later in Glasnevin cemetery, with many people present who were intrigued by this unknown man who had died with chains and cords on his body. Today, Matt's remains are venerated in the Church of Our Lady of Lourdes in Seán McDermott Street, the coffin visible through the surrounding glass.

'Never be too hard on the man who can't give up drink,' Matt once said. 'It's as hard to give up the drink as it is to raise the dead to life again. But both are possible and even easy for our Lord. We have only to depend on him.' These are surely powerful words coming from someone who knew. Ven. Matt Talbot is now a servant of God.

St Josephine Bakhita
(1869–1947)

Two children are playing in the sand dunes at the foot of the mountains in Western Sudan. Absorbed in their games, they are blissfully unaware of the strangers who have sneaked up on them under cover of the bushes. One of them comes out from behind a bush. 'Don't be afraid,' he tells the older of the two children. 'Let your sister go into the wood to get my bag.' The younger child innocently obeys.

Once the child has gone into the wood, however, two men pull out a knife and threaten her. She is paralysed with fear, unable to shout or attract her older sister's attention. The following day, she finds herself in the slave market in the local town. She has become an object for sale and barter to the highest bidder. Childhood is over.

Thus begins the life of a young Sudanese girl in the late nineteenth century. Her birth name is lost to us but her captors gave her the Arab name 'Bakhita', meaning 'The Lucky One'. Her early life was far from lucky, however. Sold several times at the market, she tried to escape but in vain. As a consequence of these attempts she was painfully tattooed by the women in the family of a Turkish general. St Josephine tells the story herself. 'After having received the order to save my sight,' she says, 'the woman began to make some cuts on my breast, then some sixty on the stomach and another forty on the right arm. It is impossible to describe how I felt. At every moment I thought I was going to die, especially when they mixed some salt into the wounds. For some hours I lay in a pool of blood, and for a while I became unconscious.'

Despite the work, the humiliations and the chains she had to endure, Josephine did not despair. 'Even as a slave, I never despaired,' she said, 'because I felt in me a mysterious force which sustained me.'

When she was sold for a fifth time, her name began to prove more apt. She was sold to the Italian Consul in Khartoum, Callisto Legnani. 'My new patron was a good man, and he wished me well. I worked as a domestic in his house but what is more, I no longer received any punishments or verbal reproaches; I was happy and at peace.' Sometime later, the Consul was recalled to Italy, and Josephine begged him to take her with him. It was fortunate that he did, for very soon afterwards the Mahadi, who were committed to converting all of Africa to Islam, conquered Khartoum.

Once in Italy, Josephine had a further short period of service before she found herself entrusted to the Canossian Sisters in Venice. Here, for the first time she received instruction in the Christian faith. Finally, her eyes were opened and she came to recognise that God 'who from my infancy I knew in my heart without knowing who he was'. In 1890, at the age of twenty-one, she was baptised and took the name of Josephine. Three years later, she entered the order of sisters who had given her refuge.

Josephine's holiness and devotion were to be seen in her commitment as a cook, gatekeeper and keeper of linens. In time, she became known affectionately among the Italians as *Madre Moretta*. She never forgot the land of her birth, however, and she travelled Italy raising funds for the missions and telling the story of her life and conversion. Her message was simple: 'Be good, love the Lord, and pray for those unfortunate enough not to know him yet. If only you knew what a great grace it is to know the good God!'

She served for half a century in the Canossians, and when she had reached her golden jubilee in the order one of the local papers wrote appreciatively about her. The article pointed out that Josephine had been announcing the Good News in the area for fifty years. 'It is she who teaches us that the secret of happiness is to be found in doing one's work silently, that peace consists in forgiveness, and that only that which is just and good is worthy of our efforts'.

Josephine died in Schio, in the northern part of Italy, on 3 February 1947. Even in her last illness, the memories of her years of slavery did not abate. On more than one occasion, as she suffered from a fever, she cried out to the nurse to break the chains because they were too heavy on her body. The people of her adopted land revered her after her death but she was not forgotten in Sudan either, where her portrait hangs in the cathedral in Khartoum.

There are several lessons we can ponder as we think of the beautiful witness of Josephine. At a time when Europe is being exposed to the cold wind of secularism it is encouraging to remember someone who came from outside of Europe to help Europeans rediscover the freshness and the vitality of the gospel. Ireland – and indeed the whole of Europe – needs new Josephines to speak to us again of the wonderful and exciting love of Christ.

Josephine was a slave for many years before she was set free. Today, it is estimated that there are twenty-seven million slaves – economic and sexual – in the world. Those who know Christ must continue to work to set all slaves free, and to try to change the conditions which make slavery possible. The witness of Josephine, in her forgiveness and forbearance towards her former masters, is a model for us all.

She had been set free in her spirit before she lost her chains.

Pope John Paul II beatified Josephine on 17 May 1992, in the presence of three hundred Canossian sisters and pilgrims from Sudan. In his homily he said, 'In our time, in which the unbridled race for power, money and pleasure is the cause of so much distrust, violence and loneliness, Sister Bakhita has been given to us once more by the Lord as a universal sister, so that she can reveal to us the secret of true happiness: the Beatitudes ... Here is a message of heroic goodness, modelled on the goodness of the heavenly Father.' Pope John Paul II himself later canonised St Josephine in the missionary month of October in the Jubilee year 2000.

BL. SOLANUS CASEY
(1870–1957)

It was late at night and the community had retired to bed. Suddenly the bell rang and the thirty friars were woken from their sleep. One of them, Bl. Solanus Casey, rose without hesitation, anxious to see who could possibly need help at that unearthly hour. He was the porter at St Bonaventure's Monastery in Detroit.

Bernard Casey was born in Wisconsin in the year 1870 to Irish immigrant farmers. Barney, as he was called, was the sixth of sixteen children. Early on, an epidemic claimed the lives of two of his siblings and permanently damaged his own voice, leaving it forever soft and feeble.

As a young adult he worked as a lumberjack, a prison guard and a streetcar motorman. It was while working in that last capacity that he witnessed an event that changed his life. To his horror, he saw a drunken sailor stabbing a young woman to death.

'To him, the brutal stabbing and the sailor's cursing symbolised the world's sin and man-made misery,' wrote James Derum, one of Solanus Casey's biographers. 'For him, the only cure for mankind's wretchedness was the love that can be learned only from and through him who died to show men what love is.'

As a result of that experience, Barney decided to become a priest but his initial attempts were not successful. He struggled with his studies, and he was dismissed after just one year. Latin and German, the languages of the lectures, proved too difficult for him.

Despite that setback, Barney still retained a deep desire to be a priest, and while praying at Mass one day he heard within him the words, 'Go to Detroit'. There, on Christmas Eve 1896, he entered the Monastery of St Bonaventure, a Capuchin friary, where he took the religious name Solanus. As before, he struggled with his academic studies, but his personal qualities were so outstanding that his superiors allowed him to be ordained, on 24 July 24 1904. Limitations were placed on his ministry, however, as he was not allowed to preach formal sermons or hear confessions. The Lord would use him powerfully nevertheless.

Initially, he was appointed to a friary in Yonkers, New York State, where he served primarily as porter and receptionist. Later he spent twenty-one years in that same capacity in Detroit. Word of his great compassion spread quickly among the faithful, along with reports of miracles. Often people would come back to the monastery and thank Solanus for healing them. 'No,' he would reply, 'it is your faith which has healed you.'

In 1923, his provincial asked him to keep a record of any healings or other special incidents reported to him. By the end of his life he had filled seven notebooks with these. They record hundreds of reported cures, the resolution of many family and domestic quarrels and countless incidences of people returning to the practice of the faith.

After Solanus's arrival in Detroit, the other brothers in the community began to notice a change in the pattern of visitors. At first, the bell would ring just a few times each day but that gradually increased and soon there were more than a hundred daily visitors. 'People might wait an hour or more to talk to him,' one brother said, 'but nobody got impatient. And he would never hurry anyone. He would listen to their story as if he had all the time in the world, and he would try to advise you or comfort you, and then he would usually give a blessing. When the people got home they would discover whoever had been sick was cured.' Another brother commented that 'it was only after death that we realised how much he had done and how close he was to God'.

Above all, it was Solanus's simple, down-to-earth manner which endeared him to people. He loved to tell and hear jokes; he loved hot dogs smothered in onions; he loved an occasional beer in the local bar – and he loved to play the violin, although that did not always endear him to others!

After twenty-one years in Detroit, Solanus returned to New York and then was sent to the novitiate in Indiana. No doubt, his superiors hoped that this transfer, as well as helping the new novices, would provide him with the opportunity for some rest. That was not to be, however. People who could not get to him in Indiana began to write to him, and soon as many as three hundred letters a day were being delivered to the monastery. He answered them all!

Again and again in his letters he repeated his life's message, that confidence in God is the very soul of prayer and becomes the condition for God's intervention in our lives. 'God condescends to use our powers if we don't spoil his plans by ours,' he once wrote. To someone who wrote to him complaining about a hospital chaplain where he had been a patient, Solanus replied, 'God could have established his Church under supervision of angels that have no faults or weaknesses; but who can doubt that as it stands today, consisting of and under the supervision of poor sinners – successors to the poor fishermen of Galilee – the Church is a more outstanding miracle than any other way'.

Solanus died in 1957. His illness was short; a skin infection had set in and he knew that he was not getting better. The day before he died, he confided in his superior that he wanted to be conscious when death came, so that 'with a deliberate act I can give my last breath to God'. On his final morning, he attempted to say something to a sister at his bedside but his voice was already weak. Then suddenly, he sat straight up in the bed and with his last breath he said, in a clear voice, 'I give my soul to Jesus Christ'.

In 1995 Pope John Paul II declared Solanus Venerable, the first American-born man to be so honoured. Twenty-two years later, on 18 November 2017, Cardinal Amato, on behalf of Pope Francis and in front of a crowd of 70,000 in the Detroit football stadium, declared him Blessed. His remains now lie in a special shrine at St Bonaventure's monastery, where people visit today in even greater numbers than when he was alive.

KAROL AND EMILIA WOJTYLA
(1879–1941, 1884–1929)

'Who will this child turn out to be?' the people wondered, as they gathered to celebrate John the Baptist's birth *(Lk.1:66)*. They had a sense that this child was special. Most families think their child is special, of course, and the Wojtyla family was no exception. Many stories are told about young Karol Wojtyla's childhood, and it is virtually impossible in most cases to separate truth from fantasy. Nevertheless, so many people have testified to one particular story about baby Karol that it should, perhaps, be given the benefit of the doubt. It is said that Karol's mother, Emilia, as she pushed his pram through the city, used to tell her neighbours, 'You'll see Lolek will be a great man some day.'

Karol Wojtyla – the future Pope St John Paul II – was born on 18 May 1920 in the Polish city of Wadowice. At that time, after centuries of subjugation, Poland had emerged from the First World War as in independent nation. It was possible again to 'breathe the Polish air', celebrate Polish culture, sing Polish folk songs and enjoy Polish theatre. It was possible once again to be a proud son or daughter of Poland. The young Karol Wojtyla would in time imbibe all of that, and make his own unique contribution.

Emilia and Karol senior were married in 1904. Before the rebirth of Poland, Karol senior had served in the Austro-Hungarian army, and he continued to serve as an officer in the new nation's army, until he retired in 1927, with the rank of captain.

Emilia Kaczorowska was born in southern Poland in 1884. There is some speculation that she was a Jewish convert but there is no solid evidence for this. Wadowice, where the couple settled down, had a Jewish population of 2,000 people, and by and large the Jewish and the Catholic residents got on well. Their younger son often played in goal for a team that mainly consisted of his local Jewish friends.

An older son, Edmund, had arrived in 1906. He was a bright young man, and from 1924 to 1929 he studied medicine at the great Jagiellonian University in Kraków. After graduation, he went on to practice at the hospital in Bielsko. Emilia and Karol were said to be justifiably proud of their first-born son.

Ten years later, the couple had a daughter, Olga, but sadly she died in infancy. A third child, Karol, was born four years later, and was known by his nickname 'Lolek'. As Lolek grew up Emilia, his mother, who suffered from poor health, was frequently ill. Nevertheless, since the family was not well off, she used to take in sewing in order the help supplement their income.

Then tragedy struck the Wojtyla household. On 13 April 1929, at the age of forty-five, Emilia died of kidney failure and congenital heart disease. Following a requiem Mass, she was buried in the parish cemetery. There has been much speculation about the influence her short life and early death might have had on the mind and theology of the later Pope but we can only speculate. Later in life, Pope St John Paul II said that he did not have many memories of his mother, who had died when he was but nine years old. On a table in his bedroom in the Vatican, however, he kept a picture of his parents, taken shortly after they were married.

Following Emilia's death, Karol senior was to be the main for-
mative influence on the future Pope. Jerzy Kluger, a Jewish friend,
remembers the captain as 'neither familiar or distant, but approach-
able'. Above all, Lolek remembered his father as a 'man of constant
prayer'. If the boy woke at night, he would invariably find his father
on his knees, silently praying. Father and son would read the Bible
together and they prayed the rosary regularly. The two would rise
early and together attend Mass at seven o'clock in the nearby church
of St Mary's. It was a routine that would stand to Lolek through the
years of his priesthood and episcopacy.

Tragedy was again to strike in 1932, when Edmund contracted
scarlet fever from a patient and died. It was a hammer blow to both
father and son. For Lolek, just twelve at the time, it was a hard lesson
about accepting God's will. Nevertheless, he learned from his father
that suffering can be transformed by faith, and that the true measure
of human greatness lies in one's character.

Karol senior's character was to be severely tested in the ensuing
years, after Nazi Germany invaded the young nation in 1939, sup-
pressing education and culture. Kraków was soon to become the
Wojtyla home. Rations were sparse and the captain's health deteriorated rapidly through the ensuing months. By December 1940,
as Lolek combined his work in a quarry with acting in a clandestine
theatre group, the father had become bedridden.

Then, one day in February 1941, Lolek returned home to find his
father had died. He rushed to the local church, where he found a
priest who came to pray with him for his father. A couple of days
later Fr Figlewicz said the requiem Mass, and Karol senior was buried in the military section of the cemetery. 'I never felt so alone,' his
son would later write. He had no one left in his family. But he had
friends. One of these remembers the young man often praying on

the floor with his arms stretched out like a crucifix, just as his father had prayed.

'Who will this child turn out to be?' The man who was Karol Wojtyla – priest, bishop, Cardinal, Pope and mystic – was formed in the school of prayer which his mother, and especially his father, brought into being. As Emilia used to say, 'You'll see Lolek will be a great man some day.'

JACQUES AND RAÏSSA MARITAIN
(1882–1973, 1883–1960)

At the beginning of the twentieth century, a young man called Jacques Maritain entered the Sorbonne, the famous university in Paris, as a student of science. A Parisian by birth, he had been raised in a liberal atmosphere in a family that was only nominally Christian, and by the time he arrived at the Sorbonne he had received a healthy dose of agnosticism. Yet, there was something in Jacques which made him recoil from the idea that there was nothing of the supernatural or transcendent in the world. He was searching for meaning in a world where meaning was elusive.

Early in his student years, he met a young Jewish immigrant from Russia, Raïssa Oumenoff. A very gifted woman, she had been admitted to the university at the early age of sixteen. Like Jacques, Raïssa found herself frustrated by the materialism and scepticism of the age, particularly as it was found among the university professors. From the start, Jacques and Raissa recognised each other as soulmates, and they quickly became inseparable, eventually marrying in 1904, while still in their early twenties. From then on, until Raïssa's death in 1960, they were constant companions.

Before that, however, in 1901, out of frustration at their failure to find a purpose in life, they had made a suicide pact, agreeing to end their lives if within a year they failed to find meaning for the word 'truth'. From that, their darkest hour, they began to emerge with a sense of hope, not least through the lectures of Henri Bergson at the Collège de France, who helped them see beyond a materialistic philosophy. Later, they met the Catholic novelist, Léon Bloy, who inspired them by his vision of life. Raïssa was particularly moved by Bloy's writings on the Jewish people and their special role in the history of salvation. He was to be their godfather when they were received together into the Catholic Church in 1906.

It was Bloy who had written that the 'only tragedy in life is not to be a saint'. This sentiment was to be at the centre of the life that Jacques and Raïssa were to live in the ensuing decades. Shortly after their conversion they took a vow of perpetual chastity, becoming Oblates of St Benedict, while remaining devoted to each other all their lives. They were united not only by the bonds of marriage but by a holy friendship, a union in which God remained an intimate third partner. They had a profound sense of the call to holiness which Bloy had inspired in them and which they saw as something to be lived out in their daily lives.

Jacques went on to become professor at the Institut Catholique in Paris, a position he was to hold until 1939. He it was who brought a new lease of life to the philosophy of St Thomas Aquinas. That great thinker had been a guiding spirit for the Catholic Church for centuries but now the young professor showed how the principles of St Thomas could be applied to today's world. Among the many topics he addressed were art, culture, democracy and human rights. Ever the democrat, Maritain was to earn the anger of the Catholic right when he did not endorse the cause of Francisco Franco in the Spanish Civil War (1936–39).

While Jacques's fame and popularity were growing, Raissa remained in the background, supporting him and collaborating with him, although she did herself publish some volumes of poetry and prose. Jacques wrote appreciatively that 'every good thing comes from God, but as an intermediary on earth everything good has come to me from her'.

The couple found themselves in the United States in 1940 but because of the German occupation they were unable to return to France. Recognised as the world's preeminent Catholic lay intellectual, Jacques continued to teach in various universities and to write on philosophical and moral issues. He and Raissa were identified with a new type of lay spirituality called 'integral humanism' which, through their commitment to prayer and engagement in the issues of the day, they lived to the full.

After the war, Jacques served for several years as French ambassador to the Holy See, becoming a close friend of Archbishop Roncalli, later Pope St John XXIII (1881–1963). In 1948, Jacques and Raïssa returned to the United States where he took up a position at Princeton University which he held until Raïssa's death in 1960.

Shortly after her death, Jacques discovered Raïssa's journals, and came to realise even more the depth of her spirituality and her intense life of prayer. He allowed them to be published in 1963. Later Thomas Merton, the great Trappist monk, called her 'perhaps one of the greatest comtemplatives of our time.'

The couple had always said that should one of them die the other would enter a religious order and, despite his advanced age, Jacques honoured this promise. Instead of entering a prestigious order like the Jesuits or Dominicans, however, he chose to join the Little Brothers of Jesus which had been inspired by the witness of Charles de Foucauld. In 1970 he made his vows as a Little Brother, living out his remaining days anonymously in a slum area in Toulouse. He died three years later at the age of ninety-one.

I leave the last word to Raïssa:

> *I have the feeling that what is asked of us is to live in the whirlwind, without keeping back any of our substance, without keeping back anything for ourselves, neither rest nor friendships nor health nor leisure – to pray incessantly, in fact to let ourselves pitch and toss in the waves of the divine will, until the day when it will say, 'that's enough'.*

BRIDGET MARY GAVIN
(1889–1966)

The session had gone well. A good number of people had turned up and there was a buzz about the place. People shared, and everyone seemed engaged except for one man, who remained at the back of the room. When the meeting was over, he stayed behind and, when the others had gone, I approached him. 'Father, I don't know how to say this but I need help … with my drinking. I am desperate.'

Five minutes later, I knocked on the door of a parishioner's house. 'Hello Father', a friendly voice said. 'Hello, Tom', I said. 'This is John, and I think he needs you.' At once, John – not his real name – was given a warm welcome and invited in. The door gently closed. John had just attended his first meeting of AA.

Many people will know about the marvelous organisation which is AA. Back in 1935, a doctor and a stockbroker founded Alcoholics Anonymous as a programme of spiritual and moral renewal for people suffering from alcohol addiction. Since then, countless millions of men and women have found solace in its self-help programme, as found in its twelve steps.

What many people do not know is that an Irish sister had a key role in its beginnings. Bridget Mary Gavin was born in Co. Mayo in 1889 and emigrated with her family to the United States in 1896. After a long journey, they arrived in Cleveland, Ohio, one of America's big industrial cities. There she found that alcoholism was a problem among the working population. Priests in the parishes had started abstinence societies encouraging young men to 'take the pledge' but they had limited success.

Bridget had the usual Catholic schooling, and ended up teaching music. As a young woman, she dated and was even briefly engaged but she felt a strong call to the religious life. She eventually joined the Sisters of Charity of St Augustine, a community that ran hospitals and schools throughout the country. She took the religious name Ignatia, and continued teaching her beloved music in the schools of Cleveland.

After ten years, however, she had a physical breakdown and, upon recovery, she was transferred to hospital ministry in Akron, Ohio. It was there that she first met Dr Robert Smith, known in AA circles as 'Dr Bob'. As a young doctor, he had started drinking heavily, and his life and practice had become unmanageable as a result.

From 1934 Ignatia began privately ministering to alcoholics with the help of a young intern called Thomas Scuderi. He recalled that 'she was a great influence on my life. She taught me about loving people'. Hospitals at that time were reluctant to admit people who were still drinking, and alcoholics were routinely sent to asylums. Ignatia realised, however, that they needed a healing beyond what medicine could provide.

By 1939, Ignatia was working with Dr Smith, whose drinking was now coming under control, and his friend Bill Wilson, a New York stockbroker. They persuaded her to admit an alcoholic officially to the hospital, and the very first alcoholic patient was admitted with 'stomach problems'. Like Rose Hawthorne in the area of cancer treatment, Sister Ignatia was breaking new ground and challenging society's prejudices towards those who were suffering.

While full of kindness herself, Ignatia's method involved 'tough love'. She required that people abstain totally from alcohol and drugs, acknowledge their need of a 'higher power', commit themselves to the AA programme and reach out to others who were still suffering.

'She saved my life', one patient said. 'I found God and sobriety through her. She loved me when there was nothing about me to love. She was AA's angel.'

Ignatia had a great devotion to the teachings of St Ignatius Loyola, founder of the Jesuits. She found a strong parallel between his writings and the twelve steps of the AA programme. Routinely she would carry around with her a small collection of Ignatius's thoughts as well as the fourteenth century classic *The Imitation of Christ*. Often she would give alcoholics leaving the hospital a medal of the Sacred Heart, telling them that acceptance represented commitment to God, to AA and to recovery. She added that if they were going to drink, they should first return the medal!

In 1952 she opened Rosary Hill Solarium in Cleveland, and worked there for another fourteen years until her own death in 1966. During her lifetime, an estimated 15,000 alcoholics came under her care and, as one author noted, 'the alcoholics' world changed.' Another admirer added, 'If the Catholic Church does not canonise her, the Protestants will make her a saint'. After her funeral, the sisters poured over 6,000 cups of coffee for those who had attended. Ignatia would have approved.

A final personal postscript is in order. A few weeks after meeting John, I got a card in the post. It was a thank-you card from him. He was doing well but taking things just one day at a time. He has a little girl from Mayo to thank for that.

ST MARIA SKOBTSOVA
(1891–1945)

Years before the fall of the Berlin Wall (1989) and the opening up of the Iron Curtain, Pope St John Paul II used to remind people in the west that 'Europe must breathe with two lungs'. The history of Europe was not just about the events that happened in France, Germany, Spain, Portugal and other nations that asserted themselves in colonial adventures in Asia, Africa and Latin America. Europe was far greater than western Europe.

Since 1989, we have been learning more about some of the heroes and heroines of the faith from the twentieth century, many of whom gave their lives for the sake of the gospel. Until recently their stories have been largely untold but we need to hear them. They are giants of faith and courage: people like Edith Stein, Titus Brandsma and Jerzy Popieluszko, to name but a few. Pope St John Paul II can also be counted among these hero saints.

The story of St Maria Skobtsova is one of these stories. It is a story in three acts, each with its own drama. Born into a prosperous Russian family, Maria's original name was Elizabeth Pilenko. A distinguished poet and a committed political activist, she married twice, first to a Bolshevik whom she divorced in 1913 and later to an anti-Bolshevik from whom she eventually separated. After her divorce, she began to question her espousal of atheism and to feel drawn to follow Christ in the Orthodox Church.

For several years, she served as Mayor of Anapa, in southern Russia, thereby risking the wrath of both left and right in the political turmoil of the time. In 1923 she left all this behind, however, and joined the myriads of people leaving Russia, making her way to Paris with her three young children. When her youngest child, Anastasia, died of meningitis in 1926, Maria experienced a profound conversion. Heartbroken, she resolved to seek 'a more authentic and purified life ... to be a mother of all, for all who need maternal care and protection'.

In Paris, she became deeply involved with the many Russian refugees who had flocked to that city. She sought them out in hospitals and prisons, as well as in mental asylums and the slums. As her faith deepened, she began to see in every person 'the very icon of God incarnate in the world'. Her bishop encouraged her to become a nun but she would only do this if she could be free to develop a type of monasticism new in the Orthodox Church, leaving her free to engage with the world without any 'barrier which might separate the heart from the world and its wounds'.

In 1932, she finally made her religious profession and became Mother Maria Skobtsova. Thus began the second act of her incredible life. As a nun, there would be no hidden cloister or monastic enclosure for her. She took a lease on a simple house in the city, and turned it into a refuge for those who were destitute. The house was big enough to contain a chapel and a soup kitchen but her own bed was a cot in the basement beside the boiler. 'At the Last Judgment I shall not be asked whether I was successful in my ascetical exercises,' she wrote, 'nor how many bows and prostrations I made. Instead I shall be asked if I fed the hungry, clothed the naked, visited the sick and the prisoners.'

During all this time, something else was going on too, similar to what was happening in the Catholic Workers' Movement in the United States. While Maria's kitchen was crowded with the poor and hungry, her living room was full of the leading intellectuals of the day. Her house was becoming a focal point for discussion and the renewal of the Orthodox faith. Orthodox Action was born, linking faith and life. 'The meaning of the liturgy,' Maria explained, 'must be translated into life. It is why Christ came into the world, and why he gave us the liturgy.'

The third and shortest act of Maria's life was to unfold with the German occupation of Paris in 1940. Her work was seen by the Nazis as subversive, since she and her chaplain, Fr Dimitri Klepinin, not only gave hospitality to Jewish people but also hid them and helped them escape. They managed to continue this practice until 1943, when they were arrested. Fr Dimitri and Maria's son Yuri died in Buchenwald concentration camp, and she herself was sent to Ravensbruck.

Here Maria managed to live for almost two years in indescribable conditions. Though stripped of her habit, she remained the mother who strengthened the faith and courage of her fellow prisoners, helping to keep alive the spark of humanity which the Nazi system tried to suffocate. 'I am your message, Lord,' she said. 'Throw me like a blazing torch into the night, that all may see and understand what it means to be a disciple.' In light of the redemptive suffering of Christ she was able to find a meaning in her own suffering. 'My state at present is such that I completely accept suffering in the knowledge that this is how things ought to be for me, and if I am to die I see in this a blessing from on high.'

In her final days, Maria performed one last heroic act which summed up beautifully her incredible spirituality. With a needle and thread, which she had purchased at the price of her meagre bread ration, she embroidered an icon of Mary holding the infant Jesus, the child already bearing the wounds of the cross.

On 31 March 1945, just days before Russian troops liberated the camp, Maria's life was ended in the gas chamber of Ravensbruck. She had taken the place of a Jewish woman, on Holy Saturday. Maria is honoured at Yad Vashem, the Holocaust memorial in Jerusalem, as one of the Righteous Among the Nations. She was also proclaimed a saint in the Orthodox tradition on 16 January 2004, fittingly in the Cathedral of St Alexander Nevsky in Paris.

BL. LAURA VICUÑA
(1891–1904)

'He does not break the crushed reed or snuff the faltering wick' writes the prophet Isaiah *(Isa. 42:3)*. Often, a holy person is not someone who has never sinned but someone who has fallen and got up again. On the other hand, sometimes a holy person is someone who has been sinned against and yet does not break. Such a person was Laura Vicuña.

In an age of license, when young people can be at the mercy of sexual predators, the life of Laura Vicuña has much to teach us about love, sacrifice and the power of prayer. Indeed, she is the patron of those who have suffered abuse.

Laura was born in Santiago in Chile on 5 April 1891. Her family were Chilean aristocrats and her father was involved with the military. Soon after her birth her father, Joseph, had to flee the country because of political upheavals. Sadly, when she was only three years old, he himself passed away.

Without any means of support, her mother, Mercedes, fled with the family to Argentina, where a local ranch owner, Manuel Mora, offered to pay for the upkeep and schooling of Mercedes's children at a boarding school run by the Salesian Sisters.

There was a catch, however. Manuel was typical of many of the gauchos of his time, fearless but unscrupulous, and he demanded a high price for his support of Mercedes and her family: she must become his mistress. Mercedes could see no way out, and she entered into a relationship with him, much to the distress of the young daughter.

In spite of that, Laura had many days of joy and peace as she grew up. As she attended the mission school with her sister Julia, it became obvious that God was doing something extraordinary in her. She had a maturity beyond her years, and she would often help the younger children with their homework and with the chores and tasks of the school. She acted almost like a mother to them, combing their hair and mending their clothing. One of her happiest times was the day when, at the age of ten, she made her First Holy Communion.

At an early age, Laura had confided in a friend her desire to become a nun when she grew up. In the meantime, she made a resolution to love God with all her strength, to do penance and to die rather than commit sin. It was a spirituality that was typical of the time, but well beyond the grasp of most children her age.

Then, something more sinister entered her life. As the years went by and the girl matured, Mora began to turn his attentions not just to the mother but also to the daughter. The first time he tried to molest her, Laura struggled fiercely until she managed to escape. After that, she learned to notice the danger signs, especially when Mora was drunk, and avoid his advances. As a punishment for her obstinacy, he refused to pay her tuition fees but the Salesian nuns nevertheless continued to educate her.

Despite her young age, Laura was aware that her mother was not living as God would have wanted. She understood that Mercedes had to look after her children, of course, but knew her mother deserved better than Mora. At this stage, Laura's health was deteriorating, and she was diagnosed with tuberculosis. Despite her weakening state, she decided to offer her life to God for her mother's conversion, and she increased her penances as time went by. With the agreement of her confessor she took private vows of poverty, chastity and obedience. Nothing seemed to change in the lifestyle of her mother and Señor Mora, however.

The winter of 1903 was particularly severe, and one day Mercedes took the opportunity of Mora's absence to take the girls away to another town, where the weather would be more clement. Shortly afterwards Mora rode into the town, demanding to stay at the house where Mercedes and her daughters were living and insisting that they should return with him. 'If he stays I will go', Laura said, opening the door and running outside. Mora followed her, caught her in the street and began to whip her. Then he kicked her and threw her brutally across the back of his horse to carry her back to his ranch. Mora realised, however, that he had been seen by some onlookers, and decided to dump the body of the young girl on the street and make his escape. Laura, already weakened by her own ill health, lingered on until 22 January, when she died of her injuries. She had not reached her thirteenth birthday.

Just before she died, Laura spoke to her mother, revealing her 'secret' to her. 'Mama,' she whispered, 'I am dying, but I'm happy to offer my life for you. I asked our Lord for this.' Mercedes fell to her knees sobbing. She realised what her daughter meant, and begged Laura's forgiveness as well as the forgiveness of God. It was a key moment for Mercedes. Not long after that, she went to confession, left Mora and became a devout Catholic again.

In September 1988 Pope St John Paul II beatified Laura calling her 'a Eucharistic flower … whose life was a poem of purity, sacrifice and filial love'. In many ways her life and death parallel those of St Maria Goretti who died at roughly the same time in Nettuno in Italy. She too had fought off the unwanted advances of a man with lustful desires. Like her, Laura did not let the sordidness of her experience destroy her innocence, nor did she allow her heart to become embittered. Instead, she prayed for her mother and for her mother's lover. Her life is a testimony to the words of St Paul, 'However much sin increased, grace was always greater' (*Rom.5:20*).

MARY MARTIN
(1892–1975)

'Gerald, I love you but I don't think I am called to marry you.' They may not be the exact words Mary spoke but her meaning was clear.

Gerald, as a young man, had gone to war, leaving his girlfriend behind. Now, on his return, he found that things had changed. Mary had fallen in love with someone else. It probably seemed a familiar story but it was not as Gerald might have suspected.

Mary Martin was born in Dublin in 1892, the eldest of a large, comfortable family. The Martins were timber merchants who had also built up a thriving shipping business. One member of the family had been the first High Sheriff of Dublin to be a Catholic.

Mary's home life was a happy one, a place where solid values were imparted in the family circle. That happiness was shattered, however, when Mary's father, whom she considered her 'rock', died suddenly in 1907. Her mother, who had given birth to twelve children, was a remarkable woman, however, and it fell to her to keep the family going and to attend to the business, which she did successfully.

Ireland then was still under British rule, and when the First World War broke out many Irish men enlisted in the British army and went to France to fight. Mary's two brothers, Tommy and Charlie, joined their number, as did her boyfriend Gerald. Mary, wanting to help and not be idle at home, began a three-month training course at the Richmond Hospital in Dublin as a member of the Voluntary Aid Detachment, where she learned to nurse soldiers who had been wounded.

In October 1915, Mary set sail for Malta where she was posted to St George's military hospital. The following year she was called up for service in France, where she was present at the Battle of the Somme, one of the bloodiest battles in human history, which lasted for nearly five months. The experience of nursing young men with gangrene, gas poisoning and limbs torn off by shells had a profound effect on Mary. It was probably this, rather than any coolness towards her boyfriend, that made Mary seek something beyond the security and supports of the married vocation.

When she returned to Ireland, after her twenty-fifth birthday, Mary knew that things could never be the same again, and Gerald knew that he would never be Mary's husband. Yet she was still uncertain about where her future lay, and in her indecision she decided to train as a midwife. During her training, she met Fr Joseph Shanahan CSSp, who was working as a missionary in West Africa. Inspired by his vision and enthusiasm, she decided to go to Nigeria as a lay missionary. Fr Shanahan later became a bishop in Nigeria, and was instrumental in founding the Kiltegan Missionaries and the Holy Rosary Sisters.

In time, Mary discovered her own true vocation and, with it, the charism of the congregation she was to found, the Medical Missionaries of Mary. Mary wanted her followers to be not only women of deep faith and prayer but also dedicated to bringing healthcare to places where there was none, and in particular to mothers, pregnant women and children. She wanted her sisters to be trained as professionally as possible. It took a lot of patience on her part to convince Church authorities – who did not envisage women practicing surgery or obstetrics – of the great need for religious women of this competence and vision.

By the time permission came, Mary had fallen ill with malaria and was close to death. Indeed, she took her first vows in 1937 in a government hospital in Nigeria. The doctor who ministered to her told her to go home and never to set foot in Africa again, but Mary was not about to leave her dream behind. She began her first novitiate in 1938 in Collon, Co. Louth, and in the following year she was invited to the town of Drogheda to take over the maternity home there. Various extensions were built to the home over the coming years, as Mary sought to build a training centre for her growing community of sisters.

Tragedy was to strike in 1952, which proved to be a horrendous year for the young order. A devastating fire swept through the training centre, virtually wiping it out and leaving 136 young sisters homeless. Fire brigades came from near and far to tend to the massive conflagration. Not daunted, Mary determined to build a hospital for the people of Drogheda, and indeed in September 1952, just a few months after the fire, the first sod was cut and work was begun. In 1966, Mary was given the Freedom of the Borough of Drogheda – the first woman to receive this honour.

In the meantime, the congregation grew in East and West Africa and later in Taiwan and South America, realising Mary's dream of offering care and medical help to women and girls who otherwise would have had no access to them. The years and the responsibility took their toll on Mary, however, and her health deteriorated between 1968 and 1975. During those years, she was lovingly looked after in the very hospital which she had done so much to make possible. Her death brought thousands to Drogheda for her funeral. The Taoiseach of the day, Liam Cosgrave, called her 'one of the outstanding Irish women of our time'.

Today, more than 400 sisters work in eighteen nations across the globe. The dream and work of Mother Mary Martin lives on.

JÓZEF AND WIKTORIA ULMA
(1900–44, 1912–44)

Auschwitz is not an easy place to visit; nor is Yad Vashem, the Holocaust memorial in Jerusalem. It is hard to stare into a room piled high with small brown suitcases marked with chalk numbers. It is shocking to see another room piled with discarded spectacles. It is heartbreaking to find another room containing human hair. It is deeply disturbing to look into the sad eyes of shaven-headed men and women in countless photos, people who would never again walk in a wood, or sit by a river, or climb a mountain or see their grandchildren. Their fate was to die in the gas chambers of the extermination camps.

In Yad Vashem, the texts beside the exhibits are disturbing as well. They remind us that sometimes it was the writings of holy men of old, like St John Chrysostom and St Augustine, that were used centuries later by people much less enlightened and much less holy to justify persecution and genocide. Yad Vashem is a sobering experience. How could people allow this to happen? Were there no dissenting voices?

It is a relief to find that Yad Vashem also has a section devoted to those called 'the Righteous Among the Nations'. These are the men and women who were not Jewish but who risked their lives and reputations to harbour Jewish friends and families from the snares of the Nazis. And there were many of them. One can find there, for instance, Elia Dalla Costa, who was Cardinal Archbishop of Florence (1931–61) and who organised a rescue network for hundreds of Jewish people in central Italy.

His story has a dramatic aspect to it, because he enlisted the help of the great cycling champion, Gino Bartali, who had won the Tour de France in 1938. To implement his plan, the Cardinal had to find a way of smuggling forged documents, made by the Franciscan friars in Assisi, passed the dangerous police checkpoints. That is where Bartali entered the story. No one suspected that the great cyclist, as he set out on his training day by day, was carrying forbidden papers in the metal tubes of his bike. Bartali too is honoured as one of the Righteous Among the Nations.

The Cardinal and Gino survived the war. But there were others who were not so fortunate. The story of Józef and Wiktoria Ulma and their children is particularly tragic. At the break of dawn on 24 March 1944, police broke into the Ulma house in Márkowa, in south-eastern Poland, and immediately shot dead the eight Jewish people the family were harbouring. Then, without hesitation, they turned their guns on the family who were sheltering them, killing all of them: Józef and Wiktoria, and their six small children, Stasia (8), Basia (6), Władzio (5), Franús (4), Antós (3) and Marysia (18 months). Afterwards, when the villagers came to bury the bodies, they found that Wiktoria was already close to giving birth to a seventh child.

Jósef Ulma was an amazing young man. A devout Catholic, he was also an innovator in many fields. He had a passion for horticulture, growing vegetables and fruit trees, and cultivating bees and silkworms. He also had a great love of photography, and his many thousands of photos survived the war. In them we glimpse Wiktoria kneading dough in the kitchen and his children running through the grass on a summer's evening. One photo shows Wiktoria sitting on Josef's lap, and it is obvious from their expression that there was a deep affection between them.

In the Ulma house, as well as the photographs, there were books on geography, an atlas and a bible. It was evident that the bible had been frequently read and, significantly, the following words of Jesus had been underlined with a red pen: 'You must love the Lord your God with all your heart, with all your soul, with all your strength ... and your neighbor as yourself' (*Lk.10:27*). Attention was also drawn to the parable of the Good Samaritan, especially the part which tells of the Samaritan lifting the wounded man on to his horse and bringing him to the inn (*Lk.10:34*).

The Ulma family put Jesus' message into practice. It was probably in the latter half of 1942 that eight Jewish people were given haven in their home. They were a cattle dealer called Szall, his four sons, two women and the daughter of one of the women. The Ulmas were probably happy to have a few extra hands around the house, and the young men helped with the tanning of animal hides. Sadly, they were all betrayed by a policeman with whom the Szalls had had a dispute over land.

In March 2017, at the request of the Archbishop of Przemśl, the diocese where the family had lived, the Congregation for the Causes of Saints agreed to remove the Ulma family from a larger list of 122 Polish martyrs, with the purpose of pursuing their cause independently. Should their cause proceed it would be quite remarkable, for the Ulmas would be the first family to be canonised as saints in the Church. In the meantime, the names of Jósef and Wiktoria Ulma, along with Elia dalla Costa and Gino Bartali, are to be found in the list of those honoured as Righteous Among the Nations.

JÉRÔME LEJEUNE
(1926–94)

Niall was one of my altar servers. He used to hold the missal at the start and end of Mass as I read the collect and post-Communion prayers. Sometimes he would sneak a little smirk at me as he came towards me. He loved to ring the bell, although he didn't always get his timing right. He fitted in really well with the other servers at the twelve o'clock Sunday Mass. I called them the 'A-Team'.

Sometimes I would banter with Niall, joking him about his bald patch, and he always gave as good as he got. Whenever Liverpool were playing he would confidently predict the score, and would then loudly remind me of it when it came true. Niall really was a special altar server, all forty-one years of him.

Not so long ago, I celebrated a requiem Mass for Sarah, a lovely old lady who passed away after a relatively short illness at the age of ninety-two. Despite early poverty and other difficult circumstances, she had lived life to the full, rearing six children and rejoicing in the younger generations too. She had much to be proud of but what stood out above all was her untiring devotion and care for her son, Damien. He was the youngest. So long as Damien was all right,

Sarah was all right. Damien needed, and continues to need, a great deal of attention, much more than my altar server Niall.

These personal stories are relevant to the story of a scientist called Jérôme Lejeune. Jerome was a French geneticist who is credited with discovering the chromosome abnormality in humans that causes Down Syndrome. He was born in 1926 in Montrouge, in the Greater Paris district of Haute-de-Seine, and after his basic medical education at the Paris School of Medicine he went on to specialise in paediatrics and genetics. He worked mainly at the French National Centre for Scientific Research. In time, he married Birthe Bringsted, and they had five children, two sons and three daughters. At the time of Jerome's death in 1994, the couple had been married for forty-two years.

In 1958, Lejeune was working in the laboratory with two colleagues, Raymond Turpin and Marthe Gautier. By studying the hands of children with Down Syndrome, Lejeune and Turpin made a significant discovery about this condition. They found that certain anomalies appeared on the fingerprints and hand markings of those with Down Syndrome, and that these anomalies already appeared during the formation of the embryo.

Lejeune and Gautier then made an even more significant breakthrough. There has been some dispute about which of them actually made the discovery but their findings were published by the French Academy of Sciences. Significantly, it was revealed that the particular defect in intellectual development known as Down Syndrome was linked to chromosomal abnormalities. It was shown for the first time that those with Down Syndrome had forty-seven chromosomes, in contrast to the forty-six chromosomes which had only recently been discovered in the general population.

Down Syndrome had in fact been studied long before this, but it was the focused research of Lejeune and his colleagues which revealed the link with chromosomes. Chromosomes are microscopically small bodies located in the nuclei of cells of animals and plants. It has been said that Lejeune's discovery basically opened up the whole scientific field of genetic disorders, a field that has been expanding ever since.

After his discovery, Lejeune started to advocate prominently for the humane care of people with Down Syndrome, and he attempted to use his findings and the findings of others to help improve their situation. He was horrified when the discovery of this genetic disorder prompted some people to abort their unborn children who had Down Syndrome and other chromosome abnormalities. As a Catholic he found this distressing.

Birthe remarked about her husband that he was a devout Catholic but was discreet about it. He prayed often, but quietly, and did not boast about his faith. She also said that his opposition to abortion may have played a role in his failure to win the Nobel Prize. After receiving one specific prize for medical research, Jérôme gave a talk in which he questioned the morality of abortion. In a letter to his wife, who was not present, he wrote, 'Today I lost my Nobel Prize in Medicine.'

Jerome also knew Pope St John Paul II before the latter became pope. Indeed, earlier on the day that Mehemet Ali Agca tried to assassinate the Pope in St Peter's Square, on 13 May 1981, they had shared lunch together. Many years before that, Karol Wojtyla, as Archbishop of Kraków, had met Lejeune through a mutual friend, Dr Wanda Poltawska, who had asked him to speak at conferences. In time, Lejeune would be invited to lead a new Pontifical Academy for Life which was very dear to his heart. Lejeune drafted the laws and oaths that each member of the academy would later take.

Sadly, Jérôme was diagnosed with lung cancer in November 1993. He served as President of the Academy for only a few weeks before his death in April 1994. Pope St John Paul II would later visit his grave in Paris in 1997 on his way to the World Youth Day. Since then, Lejeune has been named a Servant of God by the Church, and his cause for sainthood is already well advanced.

When I think of Sarah and her Damien, as well Niall's widowed mother, I am filled with total admiration for their love and dedication. By the way they have been able to say 'yes' so completely, they teach me how to love.

Some years ago, I attended a Charismatic open-air rally, at which I was one of the speakers. As the lively songs rang out, we saw a group of young adults with Down Syndrome doing the Conga through the crowd. We all wanted to join in and give full play to our emotions for the Lord, but 'self-respect' prevented many of us from doing so. Only those young adults were really free. Sometimes I wonder who has the handicap!

ANTONIA BRENNER
(1926–2013)

Can you imagine a Catholic woman, twice married and twice divorced, with eight children by two different men, becoming a nun and then founding a religious order? And can you imagine her being invited to present the gifts at the offertory during a celebration of Mass by Pope St John Paul II?

It may sound unlikely but it happened. The story of Mary Clarke is a beautiful reminder that heaven is also for those who have made mistakes, or perhaps it would be truer to say that heaven is especially for those who have made mistakes. As a wise man once said, 'A saint is a sinner who never stops trying'.

Mary grew up in an environment far removed from where she ended her life. Born in Beverly Hills, California, she grew up surrounded by the glitz and glamour of showbiz and Hollywood. The stars of the time were frequent visitors to the Clarke household: William Powell, Hedy Lamarr and John Barrymore, to name but a few. Yet, despite his success and riches, Mary's father, Joe, taught his three children to be generous and kind to those who were less fortunate. It rubbed off on Mary, though not immediately.

Beautiful and rich, Mary was an attractive 'catch' for some men, and so she ended up, all too soon at the age of eighteen, in marriage. She had three children but the marriage proved difficult and ended in divorce. Later, she married again in a civil ceremony in Las Vegas. This marriage too was to end in divorce but not before Mary had given birth to five more children.

It often happens that someone comes along at important moments in life to provide a helping hand or suggest a way forward. Mary met a priest, Fr Henry Vetter, who got her involved in the delivery of food, clothing and medicine to the prisoners of La Mesa in Tijuana, just south of the Mexican border. She threw herself into this work, perhaps remembering the values her father had taught her as she grew up. After a while, she received a contract to sell soft drinks to the prisoners, the proceeds of which she used to bail out low-level offenders.

Over the next ten years, Mary began to travel from her home to the prison, bringing not just supplies of food and clothing but more importantly a listening ear and a large amount of love. The prisoners started to look forward to her visits, and they began to christen her affectionately 'La Mama'. The warden eventually gave her permission to stay overnight in the prison and provided her with accommodation.

By this time her own children were grown up and looking after themselves. Mary had been a good mother, and she made sure that her prison visits did not lead her to neglect them in any way. Now she felt a new calling, however, a vocation to be mother to a different group of people, many of whom had never known the affection and care of a mother. At this point Mary went to her local bishop, Leo Maher, who was based in San Diego in California. He was fully aware of what was happening in his diocese and beyond, and he knew her story. Having heard Mary's plan, Bishop Leo allowed her to start a new religious order. It would be for women who were forty-five years old or more, whose concern would be for the less fortunate in society and those suffering from addiction. Mary also received the blessing of the bishop of Tijuana where the prison was situated.

By this time Mother Antonia – the name she took in religion – sold her house and belongings and moved into La Mesa prison. From now on her home was to be a cell in the women's section of the compound, measuring three by three metres. She would live in this prison cell like any other inmate, having only cold water and eating prison food. She allowed herself a crucifix on the wall, as well as a Bible and a Spanish dictionary. 'It's different to live among people than it is to visit them,' she said 'I have to be here with them in the middle of the night in case someone gets stabbed or has appendicitis.'

'La Mama' now moved freely among the prisoners, many of whom had been convicted for murder and drug crimes. Rapists, prostitutes and thieves were also present in the prison population. Antonia happily walked with them all, listening to them, touching a cheek here or a shoulder there, holding the hand of a man while he was dying. On one occasion, she even managed to stop a prison riot. She truly saw the face of Christ in every person she met, extending God's mercy to those men and women who had made lots of mistakes and who feared that no one would ever forgive them.

'Pleasure depends on where you are, who you are with, what you are eating,' she once said in a newspaper interview 'happiness is different. Happiness does not depend on where you are. I live in prison. And I have not had a day of depression in twenty-five years. I have a reason for my being.'

Mother Antonia died in October 2013, aged eighty-six, at the headquarters of the religious order she had founded, the Sisters of the Eleventh Hour of St John Eudes. How aptly named was her order, for Antonia knew that not every member of the family makes it to the table on time!

FELIPE AND MARY BARREDA
(1931–83, 1933–83)

Some older readers will remember the events of nearly forty years ago, when Archbishop Oscar Romero was assassinated while saying Mass. Like St Thomas à Becket 800 years before him, Romero fell because someone wanted 'rid of this troublesome priest'. It happened in 1980 in El Salvador, and his crime was speaking out for the poor and voiceless.

Next door to El Salvador, the small country of Nicaragua was experiencing similar extremes of poverty and oppression at the same time. Nicaragua had been ruled for many years by a ruthless dictator, Anastasio Somoza, and it wasn't until 1979, when he was overthrown, that things began to change.

Let us first go back a little to a simple couple called Felipe and Mary Barreda. They did not stand out in any way. Felipe was a watchmaker and Mary a hairdresser. Content and happy in their marriage, they reared six children and had fifteen grandchildren. They worked hard and were happy to remain anonymous. Faith was important to them, however, and through the nascent Cursillo movement, which aimed at training lay people to become Christian leaders, they became leaders in the basic Christian community in their hometown, Estreli. Their lives centred around their Catholic faith, a faith that was particularly expressed in service of the poor.

After the fall of Samoza, the new Sandinista government initiated programmes for the reform of health and literacy in Nicaragua. Although the Barredas were not overtly political, they threw themselves energetically into this work of reconstructing the country. Indeed, the revolution in Nicaragua was exceptional in having a significant level of Christian involvement; there were even two priests in the Sandinista cabinet, although their presence was not always met with approval by Church authorities.

There was also opposition to the reforms, both from within the country and from outside. By the early 1980s there was a ruthless military campaign run by the 'Contras', as they were known, which was funded by the United States and serviced by the former members of the ousted National Guard.

Operating out of neighbouring Honduras, the Contras waged a campaign of terror, targeting in particular teachers, health workers and other community workers identified with the Sandanista cause. Since Nicaragua depended heavily on the sale of coffee for its economic survival, the plantations were another chosen target. Under normal circumstances, picking coffee beans would not be regarded as a particularly dangerous occupation, nor would it be explicitly construed as an expression of Christian faith. But the Barredas saw it precisely in those terms, an expression of their support for the poorest and most needy.

Felipe and Mary could well have stayed at home, of course. After all, there were grandchildren to nurse, hair to cut and watches to mend. But Mary and Felipe heard another call. Writing to some friends, Mary expressed it well:

The opportunity to go and pick coffee will be converted into health and clothing, homes and roads and food. For this I am going to pick coffee with all the love and enthusiasm of which I am capable. Please understand that in every grain that I cut, every bean that I pick, every one of your faces will be present, the faces of your children and even the faces of those that I don't know. We wish to ask you to be present with God this Christmastime with a smile, with greater care for one another and for your children. Wherever I may be, I'll be thinking of you in these moments. I love you all very much.

Pope John XXIII would have been happy to write such powerful, human words in his great social encyclical, *Pacem in terris* (1963).

In December 1982, while participating in a coffee harvest in northern Nicaragua, the couple were kidnapped by the Contra rebels, along with fifty-six others who were involved in the work. They were forced to march to a camp in Honduras, all the while being subjected to beatings and torture. Mary herself was repeatedly raped. Finally, on 7 January 1983, they were executed. The coffee harvest itself was destroyed.

It was several months before the facts of the case became known and the fate of the couple was revealed. Their murderers were captured, and they testified to the circumstances of the events and the courage of the Barredas in the face of their captivity. Their captors tried to force them to admit that they were Communists but to the very end Felipe and Mary gave witness that they were simply Christians who were trying to help others as the gospel says. They continued with their prayers to the end.

It was said that over 5,000 people crowded into the cathedral in Estreli for their funeral, where Felipe and Mary Barreda were acclaimed as Christian martyrs who had laid down their lives out of love of God and neighbour. They could never have suspected that picking coffee would be so dangerous.

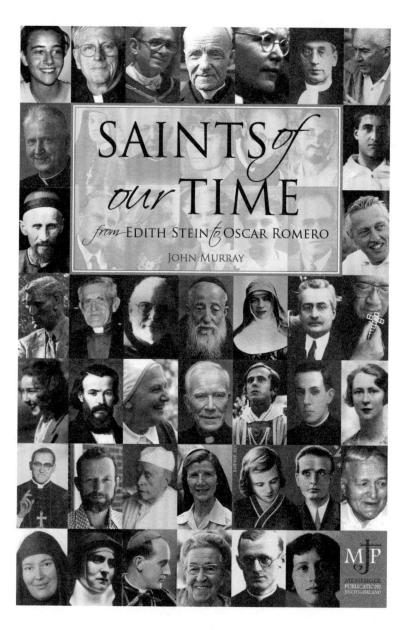

SAINTS *of* *our* TIME

from EDITH STEIN *to* OSCAR ROMERO

JOHN MURRAY

WWW.MESSENGER.IE